barcode not recognized

BAPTIZED TO THE BONE

BY DAVE JOHNSON

★

★

DRAMATISTS
PLAY SERVICE
INC.

PS
3610
.D 3344
B3
2005

BAPTIZED TO THE BONE received its world premiere at the Addison Theatre Center in Addison, Texas, opening on March 4, 2004. It was produced by the WaterTower Theatre (Terry Martin, Producing Artistic Director; Tim J. Peterson, Managing Director). It was directed by Henry Fonte; the set and costume designs were by Terry Martin; the lighting design was by Jason Foster; the sound design was by Scott Guenther; the stage manager was Sylvia May; and the the assistant stage manager was Ashley Willeby. The cast was as follows:

GLADYS .... Morgana Shaw
PREACHER .... Bob Hess
OTTIS .... Glenn Franklin

CHARACTERS

PREACHER

GLADYS, Preacher's wife

OTTIS, strapping young man

PLACE

A small country house in the Southern Sandhills.

TIME

The present.

BAPTIZED TO THE BONE

ACT ONE

Scene 1

A grandfather clock strikes nine o'clock. It is Sunday morning, just before time for church. Lights up on a living room of a modest country home. There is a small settee and an oval rug on the floor. Pictures of Jesus and "The Last Supper" are on the wall. A canvas is set up on an easel facing upstage, and a paint palette is on a small end table. The grandfather clock is upstage. There is a cabinet and mirror on one side of the room, a hallway leading to an offstage front door, a door to a bedroom w/bath, and a door to the kitchen. Gladys is sitting on the settee. She has a box of tissues. She has wrapped herself in a blanket. She has dark circles under her eyes. Singing is heard from offstage. Gladys takes out a compact from her purse, looks at herself, and then settles back underneath the blanket on the settee. Preacher enters, singing "Love Lifted Me." He is wiping off shaving cream with a towel. Gladys holds her head in her hands. Preacher is dressed in a white T-shirt and slacks. He is carrying a pressed button-down dress shirt, a tie, a vest, and a coat on a hanger. He dresses and sings. He goes on and off stage from the kitchen to the bedroom. He returns to the living room. He continues to dress and sing.

PREACHER.
  I WAS SINKING DEEP IN SIN
  FAR FROM THE PEACEFUL SHORE
  VERY DEEPLY STAINED WITHIN
  SINKING TO RISE NO MORE.

BUT THE MASTER OF THE SEA
HEARD MY DESPAIRING CRY
FROM THE WATERS LIFTED ME
NOW SAFE AM I.
LOVE LIFTED ME.

(Preacher tries to lift Gladys' head. She doesn't budge.)
LOVE LIFTED ME.
WHEN NOTHING ELSE COULD HELP,
LOVE LIFTED ME.

Sing!
LOVE LIFTED ME.
LOVE LIFTED ME.
WHEN NOTHING ELSE COULD HELP
LOOOOVE LIFTED MEEEEE.

GLADYS. I wish love was enough to lift me.

PREACHER. I hate to say it, but you look awful.

GLADYS. I know.

PREACHER. Another migraine.

GLADYS. I can't stand the thought of you going without me.

PREACHER. Now baby, we've talked about this.

GLADYS. I feel guilty.

PREACHER. The good Lord understands. You are a hard-working woman.

GLADYS. These headaches are killing me.

PREACHER. You're just going though the change.

GLADYS. I'm only forty-two. I'm nowhere near old enough to be *going through the change.*

PREACHER. You work all week like a madwoman, and you stay healthy. Then every Sunday, the only time you get to rest and the only time we can go to church together, you get sick.

GLADYS. I know.

PREACHER. You work for those headaches. You earn them.

GLADYS. Shut your mouth.

PREACHER. You work your fool self to death. And for what?

GLADYS. For those son of a bitches down at the trucking company to treat me like a dog.

PREACHER. Gladys Miles!

GLADYS. Those bastards drive me crazy.

PREACHER. I'll tell you what's the truth. You ought to quit.

GLADYS. Then where would we be?

PREACHER. We'd be all right.

GLADYS. You know better. We've always had your money from the sawmill to count on. I didn't marry a poor preacher. I married a man with a strong will and a strong back. I married a man who believed in taking care of his family.

PREACHER. I always have.

GLADYS. Well, I don't know about being no Baptist preacher's wife.

PREACHER. Would you look at this? *(Preacher examines the painting canvas across the room.)*

GLADYS. Don't look at it.

PREACHER. Look at all those curves.

GLADYS. It's not done.

PREACHER. This is beautiful. I bet you're the best student in the Baptist College art class.

GLADYS. No.

PREACHER. And imagine that. Tuition free. Just for being the wife of a man who is studying for the ministry.

GLADYS. Not so bad.

PREACHER. And there will be a lot more benefits to being a preacher's wife. You just have to trust in the ever powerful loving Lord.

GLADYS. And those turkey farmers?

PREACHER. Don't talk about them. They're good people.

GLADYS. Good enough to keep us out of the poorhouse?

PREACHER. They put a roof over our head.

GLADYS. That's about all it is.

PREACHER. It's more than a lot of people have.

GLADYS. I hate that my fate rests on whether a bunch of turkeys live or die. Those people are out of their minds worrying if they'll be able to get enough to eat. They ain't got time to worry about us.

PREACHER. Now Gladys, you're gonna work yourself up. Just lie down and sleep it off. And I promise we'll pray for you. And the Lord, as powerful as he is, will set you free from that nagging pain. *(Preacher touches her on the back of her head.)*

GLADYS. I have missed hearing you preach. *(Preacher exits to kitchen and stops at the door.)*

PREACHER. Every Sunday in August and now the first of September.

GLADYS. It's awful. Is Miss Alva Jenkins going to teach my Sunday School class again?

PREACHER. Yes she is. But she needs your prayers. Just because you're not in church this morning doesn't mean you can't pray. So say a prayer for her.

GLADYS. Why should I pray for her?

PREACHER. Before you got up this morning, Miss Alva called and confessed taking money from her mama's estate without the rest of the family knowing about it, and the whole clan wants to come down front this morning to make it public, kneel on the altar, and pray her back into the fold.

GLADYS. People stealing from their own family? *(Preacher goes into bedroom and speaks from offstage.)*

PREACHER. The devil is working. *(Preacher enters.)*

PREACHER and GLADYS. *(Slightly mocking.)* But the Lord Jesus works harder. In a mighty way, baby.

PREACHER. A mighty way! I've seen the Lord work in communities like this before and I'm here to tell ya', it is contagious.

GLADYS. Everybody's catching it.

PREACHER. Yes, baby. Everybody. You can't help but want to get right. Lord, honey and on the program this morning the twins are going to sing "Just as I am Without One Plea." *(He sings as he exits to bedroom.)*

> TO RID MY SOUL
> OF ONE DARK BLOT. TO THEE WHOSE BLOOD
> CAN CLEANSE EACH SPOT, OH LAMB, OF GOD
> I COME, I … *(Extend note.)* COME.

And when they get that seven verse song wound up, you know what that means.

GLADYS. Yes, Dave Gibson will come down and cry and beg Mrs. Lucy, and his children and the whole congregation to forgive him for getting drunk again.

PREACHER. Probably.

GLADYS. Don't he do that every Sunday? *(Preacher enters.)*

PREACHER. But this time he'll mean it.

GLADYS. *The devil just got into 'em.*

PREACHER. You know.

GLADYS. Of course I do. This is about nine weeks in a row.

PREACHER. The Lord just keeps on forgiving.

GLADYS. And the devil just keeps on calling him back.

PREACHER. Lord have mercy, that's the way it works.

GLADYS. Well, you going to get paid for your *work* today?

PREACHER. Don't you worry about that.

GLADYS. Ah, Jesus.

PREACHER. They're so good to us. They'll probably take up a

love offering.

GLADYS. Love don't pay the bills.

PREACHER. Last month they gave us eighty-three dollars, sixty-seven cents, six quarts of green beans, and three turkeys.

GLADYS. Goddamnit! We can't live on sick birds and snap beans. You need a regular paying job.

PREACHER. Eighty-three dollars —

GLADYS. You are a fool.

PREACHER. That is no way for a sick woman to talk.

GLADYS. You make me sicker.

PREACHER. I'm telling you like it is. Soon, you're going to be able to quit your job, and I'm going to be a full-time pastor at a church that's got a payroll big enough to take care of both of us. They are going to give us a parsonage, with an acre front lot with a winding paved drive leading to a front porch, with poured slab concrete finish with sanded down natural-wood-stained rockers on each end, and a glass table in the middle with fine Chinese pitchers for cold lemonade. The front door's going to have a heavy steel knocker. You'll go into a parlor with the finest settees you can imagine. Not one, two, three, maybe four covered in crushed velvet. Glass mirrors on each wall. It'll be the finest courting parlor you've ever seen. It'll lead to marble stairs that leads to a big bedroom with polished hardwood floors to a four-posted bed with Indian silk curtains surrounding it, covering up the treasure that lies within.

GLADYS. Will we have a guest room?

PREACHER. Of course, there'll be a special room just for a guest. It'll be on the far end of the house.

GLADYS. That's a good idea. That way we wouldn't disturb him.

PREACHER. Who?

GLADYS. What?

PREACHER. Who? Wouldn't disturb who?

GLADYS. The guest. The guest. You know a visiting revival preacher or someone like that.

PREACHER. Oh.

GLADYS. I'll pick out the décor for that room.

PREACHER. I thought I would do that.

GLADYS. Then I'll pick out the décor for the baby room.

PREACHER. The baby room. *(Pause.)* Sure. You can do the baby room.

GLADYS. Orange sunflowers.

PREACHER. Yes. I'm doing a children's chat about the love of Jesus this morning. You know for the little ones. You know how I feel about God's little warriors. Gladys, maybe you ought to go ahead and get one of those hysterectomies. *(Preacher exits to bedroom.)*

GLADYS. Don't say that. I'm too young. We've gone over this.

PREACHER. I know.

GLADYS. No you don't. You have no idea.

PREACHER. Yes.

GLADYS. No. You do not know what it's like to have something growing inside you and it come out dead. *(Preacher enters from bedroom.)*

PREACHER. Now.

GLADYS. I don't want to hear anything else about it. We've been saving money for a long time.

PREACHER. Twenty-five thousand is a lot.

GLADYS. How else is this going to happen? *(Long beat. Preacher looks away.)* We're close. All we need is about four thousand more and we can go up to Charlotte to the sperm bank and fertility clinic. If you go back to the mill, together with —

PREACHER. I can't go back to the mill.

GLADYS. Why not?

PREACHER. I've been called by the Holy Spirit to preach God's word. And that's what I've got to do. Otherwise I can't live with myself.

GLADYS. Well, I've lived with you for twenty-five years. I don't know why you can't.

PREACHER. You don't understand. If I ignore the call of the Lord, my life will be snuffed out.

GLADYS. By who?

PREACHER. God.

GLADYS. Ah, Jesus.

PREACHER. You don't understand.

GLADYS. I understand. You want me to forget the sperm bank, forget the fertility clinic, forget having a baby, and get my insides ripped out so you don't have to worry about it.

PREACHER. I do not.

GLADYS. We wouldn't need money for a baby.

PREACHER. You're dead wrong.

GLADYS. Who do you think you're talking to? I'm your wife. I'm your wife, goddamn you. I know what you're up to.

PREACHER. Cut it out.

GLADYS. *(Mocking.) Just get a hysterectomy. Okay honey, just get it done. You'll feel better.*

PREACHER. Listen.

GLADYS. You want me to be as helpless as you.

PREACHER. Cut that out right now and listen.

GLADYS. Did you forget? A preacher's family ought to be the lighthouse for the community. *Be fruitful and multiply.*

PREACHER. I'm worried about your health.

GLADYS. You're worried about your tuition to Baptist College. You want our savings to pay for next semester. *(Preacher goes to mirror and combs his hair one last time.)*

PREACHER. I don't want to touch our savings. I paid for summer session with my last check from the mill. My grades are good and this fall I'll start full time. By then I'll get a bigger church with a bigger payroll.

GLADYS. How?

PREACHER. I've got to get some search committees in to see me. It'll take a little time.

GLADYS. I'm running out of time.

PREACHER. We are running on the Lord's time.

GLADYS. If you don't bring home more money, neither one of us is going to have much time.

PREACHER. We've still got your job.

GLADYS. *We* is tired of working it.

PREACHER. We'll just have to pray.

GLADYS. Why don't you pray for money? How soon?

PREACHER. As soon as one of those committees comes to see me from one of the first churches over in Camden or Chesterfield.

GLADYS. They ain't no city folks going to drive out here past Hartsville to see no one horse preacher foam at the mouth to a bunch of turkey farmers.

PREACHER. They will. But I have to get through college and seminary. You just have to be patient.

GLADYS. I've been patient.

PREACHER. You're not understanding.

GLADYS. I've been patient and understanding. You've got to go back —

PREACHER. You're not listening.

GLADYS. I've listened. I've listened.

PREACHER. You're not hearing me.

GLADYS. I've heard you. Now you hear me. You go back to your job at the sawmill or else.

11

PREACHER. Else what?

GLADYS. You don't want to know.

PREACHER. But I've been called. I've been called by the Holy Spirit.

GLADYS. You're fixing to be called to meet Jesus if you don't start bringing home more money.

PREACHER. God will provide.

GLADYS. I'm the only one providing. And *goddamnit* if I'm going to be God.

PREACHER. *(To the ceiling.)* Forgive her. *(To her.) He* loves you for it.

GLADYS. I don't care what He thinks or anybody else.

PREACHER. That's not true. You sound tanked up. You've been drinking again.

GLADYS. Don't you — You know how I feel about that. I'll cut you.

PREACHER. Listen to you. Talking about cutting somebody. What kind of preacher's wife are you?

GLADYS. I ain't no preacher's wife.

PREACHER. You are.

GLADYS. I am not, because you ain't no preacher. *(Gladys exits to the bedroom. Preacher follows her.)*

PREACHER. Now don't say that.

GLADYS. It's true. You've lost your damn mind. *(Gladys enters living room. Preacher pursues.)*

PREACHER. Your tongue, woman.

GLADYS. You are just wasting time.

PREACHER. You don't want to talk to your husband like that. You need to get down on your knees and ask for forgiveness before it's too late.

GLADYS. That's horseshit and you know it.

PREACHER. We need to have a talk with Jesus.

GLADYS. Hell, your prayers'll just bounce off the ceiling. You might as well talk to a mule. *(Preacher lets her go and crosses downstage.)*

PREACHER. I can't do anything with you when you've been drinking.

GLADYS. If you say that to me one more time, I'll take a knife to your ass.

PREACHER. Save your idle threats. You drunk!

GLADYS. All I've had is a six-pack of those Red Rock, artificially flavored strawberry sodas in there.

PREACHER. To wash down all that headache medicine that you're doped up on. *(She crosses to cabinet and takes out a butcher knife.)* Put that down. Get down on your knees and let's pray.

GLADYS. For what?

PREACHER. You know for what.

GLADYS. For you to be the husband you should?

PREACHER. It's time for you to get on the straight and narrow.

GLADYS. What?

PREACHER. Let's pray. *(Preacher crosses to Gladys and takes the butcher knife from her. He takes her wrist, puts the butcher knife on the kitchen table, and she falls to her knees. He steps behind her, holds her head, closes his eyes and prays.)*

PREACHER.

    Dearly beloved master of all masters,

    savior of all saviors, prince of all princes, love of all loves

    in the name of the father of all fathers

    which art in heaven,

    whatever we call you, your disciple,

    Ezekiel Henry Miles comes calling.

GLADYS. Stop this.

PREACHER.

    We know you're going to be there, amen.

    We know you have your line open, amen.

    And tonight we have come calling and

    in the name of my poor sick wife,

    Gladys Crow Miles.

    She needs you, father.

GLADYS. You know this is not what I need.

PREACHER.

    This woman has got the migraine

    and it has gone straight to her brain.

    She needs you.

(Gladys, on her knees, turns and prays up to him.)

GLADYS. I need for you to give it to me. *(Preacher holds her head.)*

PREACHER.

    Let this woman lay down the body.

GLADYS. Yes, Lord.

PREACHER.

    Let her lay down this affliction.

GLADYS. Yes. Henry. *(Gladys puts her hand on the inside of his thigh.)*

PREACHER.

    And take up the service of the everlasting

GLADYS. Take me. *(Gladys rubs him.)*

PREACHER.

Loving heavenly Father.

(Preacher hugs her to his body.)

Oh Jesus. Ah Jesus.

GLADYS. Jesus. Henry.

PREACHER. *(Begins half singing "He Keeps Me Singing" and then switches to "Jesus Loves Me.")*

Sweetest name I know.

Fills my every longing.

Keeps me singing as I go.

(Preacher combs through her hair with his hand, consoling her and sings.)

Jesus. Jesus.

(Gladys grips his pants and her hands slide down his pant legs.)

Jesus loves me

this I know.

GLADYS. Henry. Fuck me, Jesus, fuck me.

PREACHER.

For the Bible tells me so.

Little ones to him belong.

(Gladys gives up and slouches to the floor. She holds onto the leg of his trousers.)

We are weak. But he is strong.

(Long silence. Preacher tries to look at her but looks away. He picks up his Bible and exits. As soon as he is gone, Gladys gets up and goes to the window. She watches him leave. The sound of a car cranks and drives away. She wipes her face and looks in a vanity.)

GLADYS. God. Damn. You know I tried. *(Gladys exits to the bedroom. Lights fade to half. Clock strikes once. It is nine thirty. Lights fade up. She enters pulling on a beautiful cotton dress. She checks the clock. She picks up pace. She is in a much better mood. She looks at her watch. She rushes to the cabinet and gets her purse. She goes over to cabinet and pushes a cassette tape in a player and turns it on softly. She begins to make herself up. She unbuttons the top two buttons. She throws the straps off her shoulders. She slips on her dress shoes. She puts on clip-on earrings. She washes her face and underneath her eyes. The dark circles go away. She becomes remarkably more attractive. She is spry and well. She practices walking sexy. There is a knock from the back kitchen door. She puts her makeup away in her purse in a cabinet under the mirror.)*

OTTIS. Psst. Psst! Gladys!

GLADYS. Ottis? Is that you?

OTTIS. It's me. *(Gladys goes off to let him in. Ottis, dressed in dungarees, enters with her.)*

GLADYS. Give me some. *(Robust and energetically, he picks her up, and kisses her.)*

OTTIS. For you. *(He pulls out a box of candy.)*

GLADYS. You rascal. Are you trying to fatten' me up? *(She pulls him on top of her on the settee and kisses him.)* I've missed you all week. *(He breaks from her hold.)*

OTTIS. You got anything to eat?

GLADYS. I made your favorite.

OTTIS. Fried pork chops?

GLADYS. And fried potatoes with sweet onions, turnip greens, and October beans.

OTTIS. Let's eat.

GLADYS. I'm going to stuff you to the gills. *(She kisses him.)* I hate this.

OTTIS. I can tell.

GLADYS. I mean it. One day a week is not enough.

OTTIS. I know.

GLADYS. And I can't pretend to be sick forever.

OTTIS. Try walking a mile through thick woods so no one sees you coming.

GLADYS. I know it's hard. But the last three Sundays have been the best three days of my life. *(Gladys kisses him again.)*

OTTIS. You sure we can't meet someplace else?

GLADYS. I've told you, if I met you anywhere else at any other time, somebody would find us out.

OTTIS. It's not easy.

GLADYS. I know. *(She strokes his face.)* Tell me. How you doing?

OTTIS. Not well. I'm hungry, and *(Beat.)* I'm out of money.

GLADYS. I'll take care of you.

OTTIS. You're good.

GLADYS. Well, if I can't have a baby, I might as well be *good.*

OTTIS. What?

GLADYS. Oh, nothing. It's my husband. We got into a fight this morning.

OTTIS. What about?

GLADYS. Nothing, really. We just have different ideas on how we should spend our money. It's always an issue. If you ever get married you'll see what I mean. *(Ottis crosses to the dining table. He takes a banana from the fruit bowl and eats it.)*

OTTIS. Married or not, money is an issue.

GLADYS. Well, try making plans to do something with your money, and then your husband decides there's something more important. Try a joint savings for twenty-five years. It doesn't work.

OTTIS. That's a long time.

GLADYS. You're damn right it is.

OTTIS. Has he helped?

GLADYS. With what?

OTTIS. The savings. *(Ottis saunters to her painting easel.)*

GLADYS. He's been good about it. We both have.

OTTIS. They say every couple has one saver and one spender.

GLADYS. We got a nest egg.

OTTIS. That's good. *(Beat.)* You know, every week your work gets better and better.

GLADYS. Don't look at that.

OTTIS. You've got talent.

GLADYS. Stop lying.

OTTIS. You're going to be famous.

GLADYS. Stop.

OTTIS. This is beautiful.

GLADYS. My subject is beautiful.

OTTIS. How many have you sold?

GLADYS. None.

OTTIS. You will.

GLADYS. Don't make fun of me.

OTTIS. I like abstract art and this is better than any I saw in New York.

GLADYS. That's not true.

OTTIS. Have you been?

GLADYS. I've never been anywhere.

OTTIS. You go and see. Your paintings are better.

GLADYS. No.

OTTIS. If I could take you, I'd show you.

GLADYS. I don't believe you.

OTTIS. We ought to go.

GLADYS. To New York?

OTTIS. You and me.

GLADYS. For what?

OTTIS. We could get lost up there

GLADYS. That's crazy.

OTTIS. I'd go to one of those theatre schools, and you, you could

16

take art classes with the best teachers in the world.

GLADYS. Oh, good God.

OTTIS. Then, all afternoon we could hang out in little cafes, get high on Italian coffees, go back to a little city apartment, I could read poems to you and we could make love, all evening.

GLADYS. Go on.

OTTIS. We could order up some food. Take little naps and then lie in bed and feed each other.

GLADYS. No.

OTTIS. Yes. You know, restaurants up there deliver right to your door.

GLADYS. That's crazy talk.

OTTIS. Sure it is.

GLADYS. You're serious?

OTTIS. I'm dead serious. And late at night, we could slip out to jazz clubs, drink chilled liqueurs, and come home any time we want. And if we don't want to come home, we won't. We'd be in the middle of everything. In New York, you could do all kinds of things.

GLADYS. Would you still model for me?

OTTIS. Hell, up there you'd have all the models you wanted. You might find somebody else you'd rather look at.

GLADYS. No. I'll never forget the day when the art professor at Baptist came in and said, "Today we are going to draw the male figure." I had no idea. I didn't know art. I didn't know my subject would look like you.

OTTIS. No?

GLADYS. Or that your subject could talk back. That's the best part.

OTTIS. Well, Baptist College is the most boring place in America. Where else would they make the art class models wear sweatpants?

GLADYS. I didn't complain.

OTTIS. If we went to New York, I would model things they wouldn't let us model at Baptist.

GLADYS. Like what?

OTTIS. My bones.

GLADYS. Bones?

OTTIS. Bones. Nude, naked, bones.

GLADYS. You know how to tempt a woman.

OTTIS. "The only way to beat temptation is to give in to it."

GLADYS. Oh, my God. I like that.

OTTIS. It's a quote from an Irish playwright called Oscar Wilde.

GLADYS. I like his way of thinking.

OTTIS. Yes ma'am, I do too.

GLADYS. Don't call me ma'am. *(She pushes him away.)* It makes me feel old.

OTTIS. Whatever you say, *(Beat.)* ma'am. *(Pause.)*

GLADYS. What, did I say?

OTTIS. Okay. *(Beat.)* Mama.

GLADYS. Boy.

OTTIS. Mama.

GLADYS. Boy.

OTTIS. Mama. *(Pause. They kiss.)* Mama, I'm real hungry. *(Gladys sets the table and brings him food.)*

GLADYS. I've got something for you. You are so smart. How do you know so much about New York?

OTTIS. I went while I was in college. I stayed a week.

GLADYS. You never told me that.

OTTIS. I told you I studied drama.

GLADYS. Yes.

OTTIS. One year the college sent us up there to see some shows.

GLADYS. I bet you're a good actor.

OTTIS. Actor. Director. I do everything.

GLADYS. And they sent you to New York?

OTTIS. On scholarship, the school paid my way. Of course, when I got there, I had to cut a few deals to get through the week. But I managed.

GLADYS. I bet you did.

OTTIS. This is good. I haven't eaten this good since last Sunday.

GLADYS. What have you been eating?

OTTIS. Whatever I can get. Odd jobs for money. There's no more art class modeling until school starts back.

GLADYS. Does that pay?

OTTIS. Not much.

GLADYS. How else you making it? *(Gladys exits to kitchen to bring him water.)*

OTTIS. Some guys from school and I started a company of male strippers last year.

GLADYS. Strippers?

OTTIS. It paid tuition.

GLADYS. Your parents didn't pay?

OTTIS. They don't make anything.

GLADYS. What do they do? *(Gladys enters with more water and food.)*

OTTIS. My mother works in a ball joint factory in Rock Hill. German operation. And my father, he's in sales and service for A.B. Dick.

GLADYS. Where do they live?

OTTIS. Around the state line. Pork chops.

GLADYS. What do they think of you stripping?

OTTIS. Oh shit. If my father knew, he'd do me the way he did Castro.

GLADYS. Castro?

OTTIS. Our Brazilian stud bull. Castro got wild. My father clipped his nuts.

GLADYS. God.

OTTIS. My parents don't know.

GLADYS. You sure about that?

OTTIS. I don't see them. They kicked me out. Said I had to get a "real" job.

GLADYS. Well, where do you do that stripping?

OTTIS. Columbia. Chapel Hill, Greensboro. College towns. But the company broke up. Some guys went to Atlanta, some to New York, and the rest to medical school, law school, seminary.

GLADYS. Seminary?

OTTIS. Yes. Stripping preachers.

GLADYS. Good God.

OTTIS. Now that would be a good subject for a show.

GLADYS. Who would want to see that?

OTTIS. Are you kidding? If a bunch of preachers took off their clothes? We'd sell out.

GLADYS. Jesus.

OTTIS. Maybe we could get your husband?

GLADYS. I don't think so.

OTTIS. That would be money. The truth is I miss those guys. And I definitely miss the money. Since graduation all I've really done is model for the art department at Baptist. And I did work for a little while this summer over at a sawmill in Cheraw.

GLADYS. My husband works there.

OTTIS. I thought your husband was a preacher.

GLADYS. That's what he calls himself. He was a foreman at the sawmill twenty-seven years. Now he's at Baptist College. That's how I got to take art class. Baptist will let a preacher's family take one class a semester for free.

OTTIS. Good deal. Where's your husband preach?

GLADYS. To a bunch of poor turkey farmers at The Mount of Olives Baptist Church.

OTTIS. Where is it?

GLADYS. Highway Nine, about eight miles from here. It's just a crossroad. Outside of that pickle factory over there, there's nothing. And I told Henry Miles those people couldn't afford to pay.

OTTIS. Henry Miles? *(Pause.)*

GLADYS. You know him?

OTTIS. I heard of him. I was only there a couple of weeks. I wasn't good at it. *(Ottis looks at the clock and rubs his wrist.)* I've got to get out of here.

GLADYS. What do you got to do?

OTTIS. I got *(Beat.)* to get to New York. And produce the world's first Gospel Poetry Opera.

GLADYS. That sounds passionate. *(She puts her arm around him.)* I admire a man who follows his passion. I'd give anything to a man with that kind of passion.

OTTIS. If I get to New York, I'll do it.

GLADYS. You can't do what you do here?

OTTIS. Shit. There's no need in the sandhills for a guy with a degree in theatre.

GLADYS. I guess you're right. *(Gladys brings him a short glass of whiskey from a hidden bottle.)*

OTTIS. So, go with me. *(Ottis walks over to the settee. Gladys follows him.)*

GLADYS. Oh, I can't do no such thing.

OTTIS. Sure you can.

GLADYS. How would I survive?

OTTIS. New York's a big city.

GLADYS. I'd lose my job here.

OTTIS. You won't need it. You'll find something else.

GLADYS. And my husband?

OTTIS. What about him?

GLADYS. He couldn't survive without me.

OTTIS. He's got that congregation.

GLADYS. Ottis, I'll tell you the truth. I am sick and tired of coming home sick and tired. And I have had it up my ass with eating sick birds.

OTTIS. Turkey is good eating.

GLADYS. Hell, you don't have to eat turkey every day. The only ones they give us are the ones that have some god-awful disease from eating their own shit.

OTTIS. For a preacher's wife, you've got a foul mouth.

GLADYS. It's from eating all that bird. You talk too much. *(Gladys kisses him and wrestles him toward the couch. They fall all over each other. She unbuckles his belt. He drops his pants and they get under a throw quilt. They kiss. She stops.)* Did you bring something with you?

OTTIS. Damn, mama. I was so excited to see you, I left the rubbers in the back end of the pickup.

GLADYS. Don't worry about it. Just go over to the cabinet, look in my purse, and get my diaphragm. *(He looks at her puzzled.)*

OTTIS. What?

GLADYS. Do it.

OTTIS. Do we have to use that?

GLADYS. Yes.

OTTIS. Do we need it?

GLADYS. I'd love to have your baby, baby, but it would turn out so pretty, I'd never be able to explain it.

OTTIS. Could you really get pregnant? *(Pause.)*

GLADYS. What are you saying? *(Gladys pushes him away from her.)*

OTTIS. Nothing.

GLADYS. You're saying I'm too old.

OTTIS. No I'm not.

GLADYS. I'll teach you a thing or two. I can get pregnant! *(She kicks him off her.)* The doctor told me I was one of the most fertile women he's ever seen. Get my diaphragm and shut your mouth. Unless you want to be a daddy.

OTTIS. No. No. No.

GLADYS. Maybe we should do it your way.

OTTIS. Hold on. I'll get it. *(Ottis goes over to the cabinet and opens the drawer. He pulls out two pistols and a butcher knife.)* Good God, mama. One for the preacher and one for his wife. And would you look at this butcher knife.

GLADYS. That's just in case someone comes in on us.

OTTIS. Do you know how to fire them?

GLADYS. You're damn right I do.

OTTIS. That's good to know.

GLADYS. They're not loaded. But don't worry. If anything was to ever happen, I'd take care of you. *(Gladys comes over and takes her purse from him.)*

OTTIS. You know, I'm a little short this week.

GLADYS. You ain't never short.

OTTIS. I'll give it back to you. You know I won't stiff you.

GLADYS. I don't mind if you do. *(Gladys exits with purse to the bathroom. Continues, offstage.)* I don't know why you don't just ask mama for money. How much you need? One hundred, two hundred? *(Ottis throws himself on settee.)*

OTTIS. I don't want to overstep myself.

GLADYS. You are so sweet and shy. Say one of your poems from your poetry opera thing.

OTTIS. Gospel Poetry Opera. *(Gladys enters in a soft robe.)*

GLADYS. Yes. That thing.

OTTIS. It's not a thing. It's a Gospel Poetry Opera. *(Gladys turns upstage to Ottis.)*

GLADYS. Right. *(She drops her robe.)* Gospel Poetry Opera. *(She puts her foot on his chest.)* Have you written a poem in there for me?

OTTIS.

Your eyes are like sunflowers
your ears are silk,
mama I'm coming home
to taste your sweet milk.

GLADYS. Boy, you've got it. And I'm gonna get it. *(They roll all over each other. The lights fade. Upbeat gospel music plays. Blackout.)*

Scene 2

It is Sunday night, the same day. Lights up on a pulpit stand downstage. Preacher stands in front of it addressing the theatre audience. The audience is now the congregation of the Mount of Olives Baptist Church. A hymn like "Softly and Tenderly" plays underneath his voice.

PREACHER. On this first Sunday night in September, the day before Labor Day, the day before the last day of this summer, you know Lord all of my inadequacies even before I confess them. But I'm coming to you tonight to ask that you make me a better servant for you, Lord Jesus, and that I might lead your people here in the Mount Olive Baptist community in a way that would give all the glory to you. And I come to you asking for healing for all the sick and downtrodden. I pray for Dave Gibson. Lord, release him from all those demon spirits in a bottle. I pray for Miss Alva Jenkins. Let her lay down any ill-gotten gains. And I pray for Gladys Miles, my poor sick wife, you know, Lord, with those migraines she is not in her right head. Her brain has left her body. And most of all, dear Lord, I come to you asking that if there is one unsaved soul under the sound of my voice, that you will break their hearts so they might be open to your call. Amen Lord Jesus. Amen. *(Opens eyes.)* If you walk out of here tonight without responding to the Lord's soft sweet voice calling you home, it could be for ever-lasting too late. I pray with all my being that it's not. But friends, you never know. You never know when your last opportunity will be to answer the call. You could go out on the road tonight and your life could be snuffed out. Just like that! I'm going to ask for every head bowed and every eye closed. And I'm going to ask you a question. And I'm not taking names. But the Lord knows and that's good enough for me. I want you to search your hearts. If you went out of this world tonight, would you be sure? And I don't mean would you think, and I don't mean your mother would, or your father would, or any member of your family, but I'm talking to you tonight and you are the only one who can answer this, for you. If your life was suddenly snuffed out where would you spend an everlasting eternity? Would you be sure of your salvation? Have some assurance. Jesus is mine. And he can be yours. I can't do it for you. No one here can do it for you. As the old song says, "Time after time he has waited before, and now he is waiting again." Won't you come? If there is something that is standing between you and Jesus, you lay it down at the foot of the lamb. Tonight's the night to make it right. Just one more verse. Brother Carl will you lead us? *(Music rises. Preacher drops to one knee, closes his eyes, and begins to sing the hymn. A soft light comes up on Ottis. He is in the theatre audience. He is a member of the congregation. He slips out of his seat and walks down the aisle. Preacher is still on a knee. Ottis barely refrains from going directly to Preacher. Ottis turns and slips out of the church. Preacher lifts his head skyward. Lights fade. Blackout.)*

Scene 3

Lights up. It is the middle of the next week, five o' clock in the afternoon. Preacher enters from the bedroom. He is dressed in slacks and a T-shirt. His Bible is open on the coffee table. He sits down and lights a cigarette. He sings "What a Friend We Have in Jesus."

PREACHER.
WHAT A FRIEND WE HAVE IN JESUS
ALL OUR FEARS AND GRIEF TO BEAR
WHAT A PRIVILEGE TO CARRY
EVERYTHING TO GOD IN PRAYER.

(There is a knock at the front door. Preacher panics. He quickly extinguishes his cigarette, he cleans the ashtray and hides the remaining pack of cigarettes. There is another knock at the door.) I'm coming. Hold on. *(Preacher puts on a dress shirt. He sprays a breath spray in his mouth. There is another knock at the door. He combs his hair.)* One minute. *(Preacher goes offstage to answer the door. Ottis enters briskly across the living room and stops, looking away from Preacher. Preacher slowly enters and stops.)*

OTTIS. Hey, daddy man.

PREACHER. How did you find out where I live?

OTTIS. A little lamb told me.

PREACHER. What lamb?

OTTIS. At your church. I followed you home last Sunday. You have a nice congregation over at Mount Olive. I slipped in the back last Sunday night to hear what you were up to. Didn't you see me?

PREACHER. No.

OTTIS. I'm hurt, Preacher.

PREACHER. I greeted everybody at the door as they were leaving.

OTTIS. I slipped out during your final prayer. We must have just missed each other.

PREACHER. What are you doing here?

OTTIS. This is a nice house you got, Preacher.

PREACHER. What are you doing here?

OTTIS. How about this? A sawmill man one day and a preacher man the next.

PREACHER. Yes. I quit work over at the mill and I've turned my life over to Jesus.

OTTIS. That was sudden.

PREACHER. No. I've been thinking about it for a long time.

OTTIS. When did you quit?

PREACHER. Right after you did.

OTTIS. Why?

PREACHER. I told you. I got the call to follow Jesus. I've started studying for the ministry over at Baptist College.

OTTIS. Oh yes?

PREACHER. Yes. I just finished up my first classes this summer. *(Ottis goes over and rifles through the paintings.)*

OTTIS. You've been taking art class?

PREACHER. No, those are my wife's.

OTTIS. Wow.

PREACHER. They're kind of strange.

OTTIS. Daddy man, this is abstract art.

PREACHER. I'm not sure they're any good.

OTTIS. Are you kidding, this is genius. This is better than paintings I've seen in New York.

PREACHER. I thought they were good. I just *(Beat.)* wasn't sure. She takes class at Baptist, too. As the wife of a preacher, she can take a class for free.

OTTIS. Too bad I'm not the wife of a preacher. Sounds like being in a preacher's family has a lot of perks. What are you studying?

PREACHER. My Sunday sermon.

OTTIS. What are you going to preach?

PREACHER. The prodigal returns.

OTTIS. Is that the one about a father and his son? *(Preacher walks over and sits at the table.)*

PREACHER. It's about a son who went away from home and didn't do what his father wanted. But finally the son came back home. And when he did, he was broke and destitute. And his father took him back anyway. In fact, his father killed the fatted calf and threw a big party.

OTTIS. Sounds like a good story.

PREACHER. It is.

OTTIS. My father should hear it.

PREACHER. Mine should have too.

OTTIS. You didn't get along with your father?

PREACHER. No.

OTTIS. Why not?

PREACHER. He was my father. And he was a preacher.

OTTIS. He was a preacher and he didn't know this story about the prodigal son? *(Ottis sits on the settee.)*

PREACHER. He knew the story. He preached it several times, to several different congregations. He preached it. He just didn't listen to it. But I have a feeling this sermon's going to touch someone.

OTTIS. *(Half singing.)*
TOUCH ME, JESUS, TOUCH ME.

PREACHER. Sing it. *(Slowly, with a sensual undertone, Ottis sings a song in the vein of "He Touched Me.")*

OTTIS.
WHEN SIN WAS MY NAME
AND SATAN GAVE ME FAME,
I THOUGHT I HAD EVERYTHING.
BUT I WAS SHACKLED TO A GAME
OF PAIN, AND FULL OF SHAME.

OH, TOUCH ME, WON'T YOU JESUS, TOUCH ME
AND TAKE AWAY THIS STAIN?
YES, TOUCH ME, TOUCH ME, JESUS,
AND MAKE ME WHOLE, ONCE AGAIN.
TOUCH ME, TOUCH ME, JESUS, AND MAKE
ME WHOLE, ONCE AGAIN.

PREACHER. Oh, Jesus. You're as good as any of those singers on the radio. You could sing gospel. Just buckle down and do it.

OTTIS. I'm trying.

PREACHER. Hey, how's your gospel singing thing coming along?

OTTIS. Gospel Poetry Opera. Slow. I'm having to work too much.

PREACHER. What are you doing?

OTTIS. Odd jobs. You name it. I've been underneath it.

PREACHER. I bet you have. *(Preacher walks to couch.)*

OTTIS. Ah, Preacher.

PREACHER. I'm having a baptism this week. Why don't you come on down and sing that number for us and let me put you under. We'll wash away all your sins. Get you on the straight and narrow.

OTTIS. Straight and narrow? *(Ottis grabs him by the arm.)* I don't want to be on the straight and narrow. And daddy man, I don't think you do either.

PREACHER. That's where you're wrong. I do. And I think you

should think about it, too. You should get baptized.

OTTIS. Oh daddy man, I don't need baptizing. I just want to go to New York. *(Preacher rolls his eyes.)*

PREACHER. There's not enough water in Sandy Run Creek to wash away what you're up to.

OTTIS. Ah, daddy man.

PREACHER. Of course, that's something I don't know anything about. I don't know anything about the things you're up to or about New York —

OTTIS. It don't have to be that way.

PREACHER. You need to get right and forget about all that.

OTTIS. But I have friends in New York. They say there are places up there where the men all hang out. And the rich ones have houses on the ocean, where they all sit out in the sun, naked.

PREACHER. Ah, Jesus. That sounds like some fast living.

OTTIS. It's nice. I went on a trip up there one time.

PREACHER. Really?

OTTIS. There's a place up there called Greenwich Village. It's where men congregate. They have churches that accept men like you and me.

PREACHER. What are you saying? *(Long pause.)*

OTTIS. The last time I talked to my friends, they told me there was a church of that *persuasion* that was looking for a preacher.

PREACHER. And? *(Pause.)*

OTTIS. You ...

PREACHER. What?

OTTIS. and me.

PREACHER. You and me what?

OTTIS. We ought to go up there together.

PREACHER. What?

OTTIS. I could go to one of those theatre schools, get my Gospel Poetry Opera produced on Broadway, and you could preach for one of those churches.

PREACHER. What are you talking about?

OTTIS. Think about it.

PREACHER. There's no use for me to think about it. *(Pause.)*

OTTIS. Suit yourself.

PREACHER. Think about what? I've got too much here. I can't do no such a thing. *(Preacher waits for a response. Ottis silently stares at him.)* Some men leave their wives. I could never do that. I just wouldn't ever do it. I might as well dream of winning a lottery or the Publisher's Clearing House or something. Besides, I've got a good congregation and I've made a commitment to the Lord.

OTTIS. You've layed it all down at the foot of the lamb, have you? *(He turns around and leans over the back of the settee.)* Well, as the old song says, "Time after time he has waited before, and now he's waiting again."

PREACHER. Stop that.

OTTIS. Come on.

PREACHER. You're forgetting I've got a wife!

OTTIS. I know.

PREACHER. I've got a good wife.

OTTIS. I know.

PREACHER. No, I mean it. You don't know. You don't know her. I've got a good wife. She's a good woman.

OTTIS. I'm sure … she's a good woman.

PREACHER. She is. There's probably no woman in the world that would put up with me.

OTTIS. How does she feel about you being a preacher? *(Preacher crosses to the table and sits in the far chair.)*

PREACHER. She was uncertain at first, but she's coming around.

OTTIS. Good.

PREACHER. She's just worried about how we're going to make it.

OTTIS. No different than anybody else?

PREACHER. All couples go through a money thing. In twenty-five years of marriage you go through a lot of things.

OTTIS. How does she feel about all the sex she's getting? *(Preacher looks at Ottis hard. Preacher turns away.)*

PREACHER. She wants a baby.

OTTIS. What?

PREACHER. She wants to have a baby.

OTTIS. How old is she?

PREACHER. Forty-two.

OTTIS. That's pushing it.

PREACHER. Yes. And I'm not helping things.

OTTIS. What do you mean?

PREACHER. I'm not helping things along.

OTTIS. Why this urge for a baby now?

PREACHER. There was a before. She lost it. She got pregnant. I'm not even sure it was mine. But she told in public it was mine, so I was stuck. In South Carolina, at that time, if a woman said you helped her get pregnant, that was it. There were no medical blood tests. You were it and you were married. And if you didn't marry her, the family could have you hung.

OTTIS. Hung?

PREACHER. I'm telling you what's the truth. Back then, getting a woman pregnant was serious business. So I married her to make her an honest woman. Three months after we got married she lost it. And she hasn't gotten pregnant since. And I'm telling you, I'm not helping matters at all. We've been saving twenty-five years for a baby we've never had.

OTTIS. That must be a nice little nest egg.

PREACHER. Yes, but now she wants to go up to Charlotte to a sperm bank and a fertility clinic, and that costs money. With me in Baptist College and quitting the mill it makes it tough. Money and marriage is never easy.

OTTIS. I bet.

PREACHER. If you ever get married, you'll see.

OTTIS. Yes.

PREACHER. I don't know if you will.

OTTIS. Who knows?

PREACHER. It's hard to make you, Ottis Jowers. I don't see you married like most people.

OTTIS. Man and woman.

PREACHER. No. I don't see it.

OTTIS. Man and man?

PREACHER. Neither way.

OTTIS. Oscar Wilde said, "Getting married is a sure way that you will fall in love."

PREACHER. To get married?

OTTIS. Yes.

PREACHER. That is warped philosophy. If a couple doesn't love each other before marriage, they don't stand a chance afterwards.

OTTIS. Each other? He's talking about a third party.

PREACHER. Oh, God.

OTTIS. What do you think?

PREACHER. No, no, no, I'm lucky. My wife and I understand each other.

OTTIS. Do you talk about —

PREACHER. What?

OTTIS. Men.

PREACHER. Yes. She loves men. She loves to talk about men.

OTTIS. You talk about men together?

PREACHER. We talk about a lot of things together.

OTTIS. But do you talk about men together, together?

PREACHER. Together, together. Well. Well. Well. No. No. Not in that way. No. Not in that way. *(He crosses and sits at the table.)* I just got to go on. I mean, I'm doing what's right and serving the Lord. I just can't think about things. *(Ottis crosses to the cabinet. He touches the cabinet with the tips of his fingers. There is a silence. Preacher looks away. Ottis slips behind Preacher and slowly, gently massages Preacher's shoulders. Preacher closes his eyes, takes a breath, and relaxes a bit.)*

OTTIS. How many are you going to dunk?

PREACHER. What?

OTTIS. Dunk. This Sunday. How many you going to put under?

PREACHER. Fourteen. Maybe fifteen if Dave Gibson decides to get rebaptized.

OTTIS. Big old Dave Gibson from the mill?

PREACHER. Yes.

OTTIS. He goes to church at Mount Olive?

PREACHER. Yes. Dave got married in that church.

OTTIS. Everyday at the mill he'd talk about getting drunk or getting saved.

PREACHER. I know. But once saved, always saved.

OTTIS. That fool is always down off or trying to get back up.

PREACHER. He's not a fool. The fool is one who can't see the error of his ways. You shouldn't fault a man for struggling. Fault him when he quits altogether. He just feels like he should get rebaptized.

OTTIS. Rebaptized? I thought it was once saved always saved. How often does he get baptized?

PREACHER. Some people say they've seen him baptized thirty times. I've baptized him six times myself. And I've only been preaching at Mount Olive for two months.

OTTIS. Good God.

PREACHER. Seventy times seven.

OTTIS. That's ridiculous.

PREACHER. Some people got to keep going under till they drown.

OTTIS. Dave's so big. Ain't he hard to put under?

PREACHER. The big ones go down easy and then come up floating.

OTTIS. How long you reckon all these baptizings will take?

PREACHER. At least an extra hour. I'll try not to preach so long. *(Ottis squeezes Preacher's chest. Preacher jumps up and throws Ottis' hands off of him. Preacher crosses and buttons his shirt.)* Since it will be such a long day, we're going to have dinner on the grounds, too. Why don't you come over and join us? We'll baptize you. *(Ottis coyly steps away.)*

OTTIS. Just so I can backslide like Dave Gibson?

PREACHER. No, we'll put you under right the first time.

OTTIS. You could put me under now.

PREACHER. Now you go on. I ain't got time for foolishness.

OTTIS. Foolishness?

PREACHER. Yes.

OTTIS. Is that all it is?

PREACHER. Of course it is. *(Ottis moves on him. Preacher holds Ottis off.)* It's not. *(Preacher moves to front door.)* Now go on. *(Ottis moves on Preacher harder. Preacher holds him off again.)* Besides, Gladys, my wife, is going to be home any minute.

OTTIS. I need something to eat. I'll just sit over here till she comes. I've heard the preacher's wife is real sweet. Maybe she'll ask me to stay for supper.

PREACHER. Now that ain't going to work. You just get on out of here.

OTTIS. Preacher, that ain't no way to treat a prodigal that has come asking you to pray on his behalf.

PREACHER. This ain't the Catholics. You can pray for yourself. *(Ottis throws himself down on a chair, his legs spread.)*

OTTIS. I'd rather have you pray for me. You got the power to lay some hands on me, don't you, Preacher?

PREACHER. You are a mess, Ottis Jowers. *(Laughs.)* You are a mess. *(Preacher crosses to Ottis and resists touching him.)* Now get on out of here. *(Preacher crosses back to the front door.)* You need to get to work on your gospel poetry thing.

OTTIS. GOSPEL POETRY OPERA! When people forget the specifics of what you tell them, it's a sign they are denying that what you say is real. It's a sign that they don't believe what you say is really happening.

PREACHER. I believe it's really happening.

OTTIS. Why is it then you can't remember what I'm doing? Why?

PREACHER. I remembered you were doing something.

OTTIS. Something? NO! But you didn't remember what! What I'm doing. I am doing. I am doing.

PREACHER. I know you're doing —

OTTIS. NO! I am doing. Why is it? Is it you can't? Is it? Or you don't want? You don't want. Is that it? Don't you want? *(He crosses away.)* You don't want. No! You don't want and you don't want me to want. It's not important.

PREACHER. Sure it is.

OTTIS. It's because it's not Shakespeare, Robert Frost or Johnny Cash. It's because this is something that no one has seen. It's not recognizable, so no one cares.

PREACHER. Has it occurred to you I miss the name of what you call it because I don't understand? I'm not an artist. I'm a simple preacher, but I'm trying. I'm trying. And I do want. And I do want you to want. I want! Can't you see? I want. I want you. *(Silence and awkward pause.)* Forget I said that. I can't. I know that. I know that. I didn't mean it. I mean, it didn't mean anything. I didn't mean it. *(Preacher crosses away.)*

OTTIS. Why did you say it?

PREACHER. *(Fidgeting.)* I don't — I don't —

OTTIS. Are you lying?

PREACHER. No. *(Ottis crosses on him.)*

OTTIS. Why did you take it back?

PREACHER. I don't — I don't —

OTTIS. I thought you wanted to be a preacher? I mean, if there's something standing in between you and Jesus, you have to lay it down at the foot of the cross.

PREACHER. There's nothing.

OTTIS. What's a little kiss behind the back of a sawmill?

PREACHER. I don't know what you're talking about.

OTTIS. Confession is good for you, Preacher. We can make it right, tonight.

PREACHER. Let's not talk about it. How's the Gospel Poetry Opera coming?

OTTIS. Oh, it's coming. *(Ottis smiles.)*

PREACHER. Stop! *(Ottis sits at table.)*

OTTIS. But I can't hardly do any work if I got to try to make money all the time.

PREACHER. You shouldn't have to work.

OTTIS. I'm living out of the back end of my pickup. But, I have set it up kind of nice. You ought to come out and visit me. How about Saturday night, say sometime after dark.

PREACHER. I don't know about that.

OTTIS. Come on, daddy man. I get lonely out there. I don't see anyone.

PREACHER. I'm sure you have a friend.

OTTIS. All my friends moved away to cities or back to where they came from or something. And my family has thrown me out for good.

PREACHER. That's terrible *(Long beat. Preacher crosses and stands behind Ottis.)* Could you say one of your poems for me?

OTTIS. I don't feel like it.

PREACHER. I always liked to hear you talk about poetry and theatre.

OTTIS. You were pretty good about listening to me.

PREACHER. At the mill, the first time you talked about it, you were embarrassed. You were afraid the boys would think you were too educated. Too much of a college boy.

OTTIS. Too much of a queer.

PREACHER. Now. The boys liked you.

OTTIS. They didn't make fun of me?

PREACHER. We liked you. We hated to see you quit.

OTTIS. I wasn't cut out for a sawmill.

PREACHER. Say one of your poems, before you have to go.

OTTIS. I can't think of any. *(Ottis crosses downstage.)*

PREACHER. You're your own man. I understand. Heaven knows you're going to do what you want to do. *(Preacher crosses and sits on the settee.)*

OTTIS. I'll say one. But before I do, tell me one thing. Why did you quit your job to be a preacher?

PREACHER. *(Long beat.)* You know.

OTTIS. I call this one "Daddy Man." It's sort of a Southern haiku.

PREACHER. High what?

OTTIS. Haiku. A haiku is a three-line poem. It's Japanese. "Daddy Man." *(Clears his throat.)*

> Your eyes, sunflowers
> your ears, silk,
> I'm coming home, daddy man, to taste your sweet milk.

PREACHER. Ah, Jesus. *(Ottis puts his hand on Preacher's hand. Ottis takes Preacher's hand and puts it on his thigh. Preacher hears a car arriving. Preacher jumps up and runs to the door.)* OTTIS! *(Preacher crosses back to Ottis.)* You've got to get out of here!

OTTIS. I need something to eat.

PREACHER. Here take this. Thirty dollars. Now go on.

OTTIS. All right, daddy man. *(Ottis pulls Preacher close to him. The Bible falls to the floor. Ottis quickly kisses him. Preacher fidgets and then finally pushes him away. Ottis slides out the back door.)*

PREACHER. *(Loud whisper.)* Next time, *(As the kitchen door swings closed, Gladys enters. Gladys and Ottis do not see each other. Gladys startles Preacher.)* not so late in the day!

GLADYS. Who are you talking to? *(Gladys stops and examines the room.)*

PREACHER. I'm just —

GLADYS. Just what?

PREACHER. Praying.

GLADYS. For that job I hope.

PREACHER. For the Lord to provide. How was your day?

GLADYS. I don't want to talk about it. Those son of a bitches down at the trucking company tried to fire me. *(Preacher blocks the kitchen door. Gladys pushes him out of the way to get through.)* Do you believe this shit? They told me they weren't getting their checks fast enough. I said you pay me a decent wage and you'll get your checks faster. *(Gladys enters from kitchen with a red soda. She crosses to settee. Takes off her shoes and strips off her pantyhose. She sprawls out.)* They make enough money to choke this whole town. They could pay me. Sometimes they forget, that the payroll supervisor writes and signs her own check.

PREACHER. Let's not let temptation get the best of us. The Bible warns us. Don't forget The Word.

GLADYS. I'm not forgetting The Word. I know what it says. What, you think that's the only book?

PREACHER. No.

GLADYS. I know a thing or two. I know some Wilde man once wrote that giving in to temptation might just get it out of the way.

PREACHER. Some wild man?

GLADYS. A playwright.

PREACHER. When have you ever seen a play? *(Preacher sits beside Gladys and begins rubbing her feet.)*

GLADYS. I've seen a lot. I'm not as foolish as you think. What I'm saying is, I ought to just give in to the devil and just get it over with. That way I wouldn't have to worry about it.

PREACHER. That's blasphemy. That's denying the power of heaven.

GLADYS. I know, but I could kill them.

PREACHER. With kindness, baby. Kill them with kindness.

GLADYS. Kindness? Shit. That boss man is the meanest son of a bitch I have ever seen. I swear, the devil ain't never asked no man to be that mean. I'd like to fill T.E. Demby's ass full of buckshot.

(Pause.) Are you OK?

PREACHER. I'm fine.

GLADYS. You look like a scared possum.

PREACHER. What?

GLADYS. Are you sick?

PREACHER. Why?

GLADYS. You look like you're about to miss your bus. *(Gladys begins searching through the house.)*

PREACHER. What are you doing?

GLADYS. Something's not right around here.

PREACHER. What?

GLADYS. *(Offstage.)* Is someone in this house?

PREACHER. What?

GLADYS. *(Reenters.)* You're up to something.

PREACHER. What?

GLADYS. Is there another woman in here?

PREACHER. What are you talking about?

GLADYS. You heard me.

PREACHER. What? *(Gladys exits to kitchen, searching.)*

GLADYS. Are you keeping a Betty on the side?

PREACHER. God, no! *(Gladys enters living room.)*

GLADYS. You look suspicious.

PREACHER. What is wrong with you?

GLADYS. I don't want to find out anything.

PREACHER. Stop looking.

GLADYS. Because you always hear these crazy stories about preachers and their secretaries and mess like that. *(Gladys exits to bedroom.)*

PREACHER. I don't have a secretary.

GLADYS. Do you want one?

PREACHER. It would be nice —

GLADYS. What?

PREACHER. It would be good — *(Gladys enters living room.)*

GLADYS. What?

PREACHER. NO! No! I don't need one. I was just saying if some things needed to be done like typing the church bulletin and the program for the week, it would be nice to have help. But I don't need a secretary like that.

GLADYS. There better not be another woman, because you know what I'll do.

PREACHER. I have been reading The Word of the Lord all day.

GLADYS. What the hell is The Word of the Lord doing turned

35

upside down in the middle of the floor?

PREACHER. It must have fallen off the table. *(Preacher goes to pick it up.)*

GLADYS. Yes?

PREACHER. Yes! I was cooking supper for us, and I was in here studying, and then I smelled something burning and ran into the kitchen.

GLADYS. Did! Did you?

PREACHER. Yes. *(Gladys sniffs him.)* Woman, what are you doing?

GLADYS. I just want to get a nose full of you.

PREACHER. You are out of your mind. *(Gladys grabs the crotch of his trousers.)*

GLADYS. What's for supper?

PREACHER. Irish potatoes, hoe cake, and October beans.

GLADYS. You lying to me? *(She squeezes him. He winces and resists.)*

PREACHER. No.

GLADYS. I hope not. *(Preacher pulls away and exits to kitchen. Gladys falls down on the settee, exasperated. Blackout.)*

Scene 4

It is three days later, Saturday night. Slow, sultry gospel music plays. Dim blue lights rise on downstage right. Ottis is sitting on the hood of his pickup truck. There is a blanket and pillow on top of a small mattress. Ottis is loading a pistol and taking aim at a target out into the darkness. He takes a drink of whiskey. He practices drawing the gun from his pants. He polishes the pistol and puts it inside the truck. In a dim silhouette Preacher steps into the light, near where Ottis waits. Ottis sees him, picks up the bottle of whiskey and hands it to Preacher.

Preacher takes a drink. Ottis takes bottle, puts it down and steps into the middle of his mattress. They look at each other. Preacher follows. Then slowly and deliberately Ottis steps up and puts his hands on Preacher's waist. Ottis gently kisses Preacher. Ottis slips easily out of his shirt. Ottis places Preacher's hand on his chest. Preacher is shy and nervously

36

resistant. Ottis then helps Preacher out of his shirt. Ottis slowly kisses Preacher softly on the neck. Preacher can barely contain himself. Preacher can no longer resist. The lights fade down and the music rises. Blackout.

End of Act One

ACT TWO

Scene 1

Lights up. It is the next day, Sunday morning. Gladys is asleep on the settee of the living room. It is quiet. There is a knock at the front door.

OTTIS. Gladys. Gladys! *(Gladys wakes.)*

GLADYS. Ottis? *(Gladys exits to let him in.)*

OTTIS. Hey, mama.

GLADYS. Where have you been? *(Gladys and Ottis enter fully.)* I didn't think you were coming.

OTTIS. Things got busy.

GLADYS. I don't have any way to get hold of you. And it's late.

OTTIS. I'm sorry about that.

GLADYS. My husband went to church over an hour ago.

OTTIS. I slept late.

GLADYS. Saturday night catting with another woman?

OTTIS. You're keeping me on a short leash.

GLADYS. It's the only way to keep a pit bull mean.

OTTIS. Keep him close enough, he'll bite you.

GLADYS. Now you're talking.

OTTIS. Mama, you're a mess.

GLADYS. It doesn't matter. I can't be jealous. I know you have a girlfriend. *(Pause.)* You should. I don't know why a young man like you would want to be with a woman like me.

OTTIS. You're beautiful. You're tough. And you know what you're doing.

GLADYS. I'm doing you, you crazy poet.

OTTIS. Crazy poet?

GLADYS. Yes. How's your poetry singing thing coming on.

OTTIS. Gospel Poetry Opera.

GLADYS. I'm sorry. Tell me what it is then, exactly.

OTTIS. Imagine Shakespeare. He wrote plays. Sometimes in the plays the characters perform a play. It is known as a play within a play.

GLADYS. Okay.

OTTIS. It would be as if you painted a painting of someone painting a painting.

GLADYS. Okay.

OTTIS. The Gospel Poetry Opera is a lyrical poem in a gospel song ...

GLADYS. Oh.

OTTIS. ... in an aria, in a play, in a grand opera.

GLADYS. Sounds good.

OTTIS. It is good.

GLADYS. When can I see it?

OTTIS. I don't have enough time to even finish it. I'm always worried about making money. But with all this pressure coming from everywhere, I can hardly hold a pencil long enough to write a decent sentence.

GLADYS. Write them with your wigger. You keep that up pretty good.

OTTIS. Is that all you ever think about?

GLADYS. I just like for you to give me a hard time. *(Long beat. They look at each other and laugh.)* Serious. You can do anything you want. Ottis Jowers, don't you ever let anybody tell you, you can't. Do you hear me? *(Ottis nods.)*

OTTIS. You know, my mother thinks I've lost my mind.

GLADYS. Well you haven't.

OTTIS. I'm living full time now in the back of the pick-up. She won't even let me back in the house to bathe.

GLADYS. When was the last time? *(Ottis looks down. Long beat.)* Where are you parking your truck?

OTTIS. Over near Julian Jenkins' lake.

GLADYS. Upwind from that turkey house, I hope.

OTTIS. Yes.

GLADYS. Boy, you're living a poetic life.

OTTIS. I wouldn't call it that.

GLADYS. You are. You are making poems of your life.

OTTIS. Hardly.

GLADYS. The words will come. I know it. I can't help saying it. *(Pause.)* You will get up, get out of here, and go up to New York City. *(Long beat.)*

OTTIS. With what?

GLADYS. I could write you a check. *(Beat.)*

OTTIS. What about *(Beat.)* the preacher?

GLADYS. The preacher? *(They look directly at each other. Long pause.)* What I'm talking about has nothing to do with the preacher. *(Beat.)* I don't know why you would worry about him.

OTTIS. Just wondered.

GLADYS. Wondered what?

OTTIS. Nothing. How's he's doing.

GLADYS. How he's doing? You know what I like about you most?

OTTIS. No.

GLADYS. You're strong but sweet.

OTTIS. What?

GLADYS. You're making love to me and you still show concern for my husband. That's a rare quality.

OTTIS. You think? *(Gladys gets up and moves behind the settee.)*

GLADYS. Shit, he's a dreamer.

OTTIS. Yes?

GLADYS. He works hard, but he's a dreamer. He's always *telling me like it is.* How I'm going to soon be able to quit my job and he's going to be a full-time pastor at a church that's got a payroll big enough to take care of both of us. They are going to give us a parsonage with an acre front lot with a winding paved drive. No more of this living two and a half miles off the paved highway. He says our driveway will be leading to a front porch with poured slab concrete finish with sanded down natural-wood-stained rockers on each end, a glass table in the middle with fine Chinese pitchers for cold lemonade. And then he tells about the front door that's going to have a heavy steel knocker. And you'll be able to go into a parlor with the finest settees you can imagine. Not one, two, three, maybe four covered in crushed velvet. Glass mirrors on each wall. It'll be the finest courting parlor you have ever seen. *(Becoming slow and deliberate, she moves and sits beside him.)* That leads to marble stairs that leads to a big bedroom with polished hardwood floors to a four-posted bed with Indian silk curtains surrounding it covering up the hidden treasure that lies within. *(Long pause.)* That's me. *(Pause.)*

OTTIS. I know. *(Gladys steps away from Ottis.)*

GLADYS. He's a good man. He works for what he believes in. But the truth is he's just an ex-mill foreman who dreams of being a big-time preacher. Somebody that matters to somebody. Neither one of those somebodies is me.

OTTIS. That's not true.

GLADYS. How do you know?

OTTIS. By how worked up you all get when you talk about each other. *(Ottis recognizes his slip and bites his tongue. Gladys pauses slightly but continues.)*

GLADYS. He was up all night. I fell asleep. He had to prepare for a baptizing today.

OTTIS. Oh?

GLADYS. He hadn't even come to bed when I got up.

OTTIS. Mmm.

GLADYS. He has about fifteen people to baptize today. He won't be home for awhile. He didn't come to bed last night. He's stayed up late to study, but he's never not come to bed. He doesn't do that. *(Gladys leans into Ottis.)* You alright?

OTTIS. Me? Sure.

GLADYS. You look like you wrestled the devil all night yourself. You need some money? *(Gladys pulls out a wad of dollars from the inside of her underwear.)* Take it. *(Gladys puts the money down his shirt.)*

OTTIS. You know I appreciate it.

GLADYS. Your mother's only got one son. She ought not forget it. Go wash up? *(Gladys pushes Ottis off. Softly, almost childlike, Ottis exits to the bedroom and bath. Gladys crosses to the cabinet and mirror. She speaks to it and brushes her hair.)* I'm not getting one day prettier. *(The shower begins running.)* I say if you can get out of here you should do it. If you got ideas you should act on them. *(Gladys walks into the doorway and speaks to Ottis.)* Don't let anyone stand in your way. And I can tell you, your own people, no matter who you are and where you come from, will try to kill you and anything you stand for. It's either you or them. If my son had been born alive, this week, he'd be twenty-five years old. *(Gladys exits to the kitchen.)* I can guarantee you I would've raised him good. I would have sent him off to the best school I could find. *(The shower stops. Gladys does not hear the sound of a car arriving.)* And if he wanted to be a doctor or a lawyer that would be fine. But to have a son who wanted to write a Gospel Poetry Opera, that would be something. *(Preacher enters with bags of groceries without being noticed. He hears Gladys speaking from the kitchen.)* If that baby had just been born alive. I would have gotten my son the hell out of here, I can tell you that. *(Gladys enters with a red soda.)* OOOH Jesus!! You scared me. Why are you sneaking up on me like that?

PREACHER. Relax.

GLADYS. I can't relax. *(Getting louder.)* Mr. Preacher, always telling everyone how to live. *(Gladys steps in front of the bedroom door.)*

PREACHER. Stop the nonsense. I know you wanted that baby. And if we had it, you're right, you would have been a good mother. *(Pause.)* We prayed for you today.

GLADYS. What are you doing home so early?

PREACHER. I forgot to check the creek this week. We haven't had any rain in so long that it was too shallow. The water wasn't deep enough to dunk them all the way under.

GLADYS. Couldn't you have sprinkled them or done it indoors or something like that? *(Preacher takes groceries into kitchen.)*

PREACHER. No. That wouldn't do. You know that. *(Preacher enters with a red soda.)* These old time Baptists don't even have an indoor baptistery. They believe you have to go down to the creek and do it the natural way.

GLADYS. You could go back and pour water on their heads or something.

PREACHER. Woman, what are you thinking? We ain't no Methodists. You know you can't sprinkle or pour water on them.

GLADYS. Why not? *(Preacher sits on the settee.)*

PREACHER. How long have you been a Baptist? There ain't but one way to get cleansed from all your sin. All the way under.

GLADYS. Yes. Honey, could you go in the kitchen and heat up those leftovers? I've been feeling better and I am ready to eat. *(Gladys pulls him up off the settee.)*

PREACHER. That's a switch.

GLADYS. I am starving.

PREACHER. Usually with these migraines you can't eat.

GLADYS. Right now I could eat your ass.

PREACHER. If you did you would fleshen' up. *(She pushes him off into the kitchen.)* You better get back under those covers.

GLADYS. Don't worry. *(Ottis enters dressed and clean with a towel over his arm.)*

OTTIS. I've been thinking.

GLADYS. You got to get out. He's here.

OTTIS. I need more money.

GLADYS. I gave you a lot.

OTTIS. I can't make it too long on that. *(Ottis sits down at the table. She goes to her purse and gives him another wad of money.)*

GLADYS. Here goddamnit. Take it! *(She takes the towel from him and throws it behind the cabinet.)* Go.

PREACHER. *(Off.)* Baby, did you say something?

GLADYS. I said reheat those October beans, and there's some pot roast in there. *(Ottis counts the money.)*

OTTIS. That sounds good.

GLADYS. Damn it. You can count it later. Please, get out.

OTTIS. If I'm going to get to New York, I'm going to need more.

GLADYS. I'll get more, a lot more. I swear to God.

OTTIS. Where?

GLADYS. I told you, I'll get it. Trust me.

OTTIS. When?

GLADYS. Next Sunday. You know how I feel. *(Ottis stops counting.)*

OTTIS. I need it now.

PREACHER. *(Offstage, but closer.)* Honey. *(Ottis does not move. Gladys panics, springs to the cabinet, and pulls a gun. Ottis doesn't see it. Preacher enters, holding a couple cans of vegetables. Gladys spins around and hides the gun behind her. Preacher doesn't see the gun.)* Who are you talking to?

OTTIS. Preacher? You are the preacher? *(Pause.)*

PREACHER. Aaah. *(Long pause.)*

GLADYS. This is the preacher.

OTTIS. Good. Good. Good. *(Ottis crosses to Preacher and offers his hand. Preacher doesn't take it.)* I am Ottis. Ottis Jowers. *(Ottis crosses to exactly halfway between Gladys and Preacher.)* I am here to con-fess something.

PREACHER and GLADYS. What?

OTTIS. My sins. I want to get right. *(Ottis crosses and sits on the settee.)*

PREACHER. Son, we are in the middle of Sunday dinner right now.

OTTIS. And I am sorry as I can be. From the bottom of my heart I am. But I feel now is the time. I want to lay all my burdens down here and now.

PREACHER. How did you get in here?

OTTIS. Your lovely wife invited me in.

PREACHER. I didn't hear you come in.

GLADYS. I let him in.

PREACHER. I think you ought to come down to the church next Sunday. That's what I think.

OTTIS. But preacher, what if I was to go out on the road tonight and my life was to get snuffed out? What if I was to die tonight and go out into an everlasting eternity without getting myself right? Wouldn't you feel like the devil himself?

PREACHER. Son, the Lord sometimes grants us things.

OTTIS. I can't wait.

PREACHER. Gladys, I'm sorry, baby, but I'm going to have to ask you to leave us alone for a minute. *(Preacher crosses to her.)* If I am going to get this young man right with the Lord, I think we will need some privacy.

GLADYS. NO. I'm staying right here.

PREACHER. Please, baby, this is no work for a woman to see.

GLADYS. Where three are gathered together, there he shall be also.

PREACHER. Now is not the time for Scripture.

GLADYS. Isn't he trying to get saved?

PREACHER. Let me handle this.

GLADYS. But I've been sick. I haven't seen anyone get saved in a long time. No. I'm staying to see this one. *(Preacher crosses downstage.)*

OTTIS. Mama. *(Beat.)* Mary, Joseph, and Jesus. Ma'am. I do respect you've been ill and you wish to see your man doing his godly work but —

PREACHER. He's right. To cast out demons you got —

OTTIS. Demons?

PREACHER. Yes. I can tell we need to cast out some demons.

OTTIS. What demons?

PREACHER. You are full of them.

OTTIS. What?

PREACHER. You can tell by looking at you.

OTTIS. I ain't full of demons. Now you wait just a goddamn minute. *(Preacher crosses to Gladys.)*

PREACHER. See, baby, how he's started taking the Lord's name in vain. Go to the kitchen.

GLADYS. I will not. *(Gladys squeezes the gun. Preacher, in a very short space, circles upstage, a quick 360-degree turn.)*

PREACHER. Woman, leave!

OTTIS. Please ma'am. Honestly, I ask you. In God's name.

GLADYS. God's name. All right, but just a minute. I'll be right in there. *(No one moves. Gladys reluctantly goes to the kitchen. While hiding her gun, she crosses upstage of Preacher and Ottis.)*

PREACHER. Are you out of your mind?

OTTIS. I just came to get my demons out.

PREACHER. You know you're not supposed to come up in here on the weekends.

OTTIS. I couldn't wait to see you.

PREACHER. Oh, Ottis, that's really sweet, but this is trouble. Real trouble.

OTTIS. Daddy man. I'm broke.

PREACHER. I gave you money last night.

OTTIS. How much did those poor turkey farmers take up for their loving pastor today?

PREACHER. I can't give you one red cent of it.

OTTIS. If you want me to write any more poems for you, I'll need some more money.

PREACHER. Go!

OTTIS. I tell you, Preacher, I am in bad need of confessing. *(Preacher reaches in his pocket.)*

PREACHER. Here! Now get out.

OTTIS. I know they love their preacher more than this.

PREACHER. Well that's all I can give you.

OTTIS. My soul is on fire to tell the truth. Maybe the spirit muse will hit me and I'll have to recite one of my poems. *(Preacher pulls out another wad of cash from the other pocket.)*

PREACHER. That's all I've got. Please leave. You don't know my wife. She will shoot both of us. *(Ottis throws himself on the floor, wraps his arms around Preacher's waist, and hugs him.)*

OTTIS. But you know my old man threw me out. I don't have anywhere to live. And how am I ever going to get to New York without any money, daddy man?

PREACHER. I'll find some more money. Come back in the middle of the week, when my wife's not here. Don't do this to me. You know how I feel. Just leave before it's too late. *(Ottis, on his knees, shakes his head "no." Preacher turns and crosses to the cabinet and spins around with a gun drawn on Ottis. Ottis jumps to his feet and throws his hands up.)*

OTTIS. Ah, shit! *(Gladys bursts in with her gun drawn. Ottis steps back.)* Ah, shit!

GLADYS. What the hell is going on in here? *(Gladys stares at Ottis and then turns to see Preacher with his gun drawn on Ottis as well. Both Preacher and Gladys are bewildered.)*

PREACHER. Gladys, what the hell are you doing?

GLADYS. What the hell are you doing? *(They both turn to Ottis.)*

OTTIS. I was just trying to confess. Get on the straight and narrow. Get baptized. You know. All the way under. *(Ottis puts his hands down and crosses upstage. Preacher crosses downstage with a gun on Ottis. Gladys holds her gun on Ottis.)* Preacher, you were right, my demons can wait. *(To Gladys.)* Ma'am, I do thank you for the warm invitation for Sunday dinner. I'll take you up some other time. Real soon. *(Backs toward door.)* How about a poem? *(Preacher is downstage, and Gladys is upstage, both across stage from Ottis. Both*

45

Preacher and Gladys stand at attention, holding their pistols on Ottis.)
     Your eyes are sunflowers
     your ears are silk
     the prodigal's come home
     to a preacher, his wife
     two *unloaded* guns,
(Ottis reaches into the cabinet and pulls out the butcher knife. Gladys fires her pistol into the air and then points it at Ottis. Preacher reacts and fires his pistol in the air and then points his pistol at Gladys. Ottis turns and moves on Preacher with the butcher knife.) Are you out of your fucking mind? *(Gladys fires her pistol in the air again and again points her pistol at Ottis. Ottis stops. Ottis turns and moves toward Gladys with the butcher knife. Gladys holds the gun on Ottis. When Ottis gets close to Gladys, Preacher takes his pistol off Gladys, fires it into the air and then aims his pistol at Ottis. Gladys takes her pistol off Ottis, fires it into the air and turns it on Preacher. Long pause. They all exchange looks and then Gladys and Preacher both turn their pistols on Ottis. Ottis backs away.)* I take it you all don't support the arts. *(Gladys and Preacher squeeze their pistols harder and take a step toward him. Ottis lays down the butcher knife, He slowly backs to the door, never taking his eyes off them. He turns quickly and is gone. Gladys and Preacher are left holding their pistols. They look at the empty doorway. They look at each other. Blackout.)*

Scene 2

Lights up. It is the middle of the next week. Ottis is sitting across the table from Preacher.

PREACHER. I was afraid you wouldn't see me again.

OTTIS. Could you blame me. Everybody in the house shooting off. I don't know what kind of juice you two run on around here.

PREACHER. I'm sorry. You know I wouldn't hurt you.

OTTIS. You didn't have any problem firing pistols on me. You think I was born yesterday?

PREACHER. I'm sorry. Don't misunderstand us. Gladys is a good woman. She just drinks a little too much. *(Ottis crosses downstage.)*

OTTIS. A drunk preacher's wife? Do you expect me to believe that? That's about as cliché as it gets.

PREACHER. Stop it.

OTTIS. What did you two say to each other after I left?

PREACHER. Nothing.

OTTIS. Nothing?

PREACHER. We haven't talked about it.

OTTIS. What is this, Wednesday? Three days and you haven't even brought it up?

PREACHER. I know it's odd.

OTTIS. You better believe it is. Two people shooting up their own goddamn house in front of a stranger and you don't even discuss it?

PREACHER. I know. *(Ottis sits on the settee.)*

OTTIS. Let's hurry this up. I don't want your wife coming in here on me. *(Preacher crosses and sits on the settee.)*

PREACHER. I am glad you're here. I wouldn't have blamed you for never coming back.

OTTIS. I'm a fool. I couldn't resist.

PREACHER. I've got money.

OTTIS. Sure you do. I've heard enough.

PREACHER. No. I've got a way out. Resources.

OTTIS. Cash?

PREACHER. From the bank. I'm going down to the bank on Friday to get money. Then you and I can leave town.

OTTIS. You and I?

PREACHER. New York. I'm going with you.

OTTIS. You are?

PREACHER. Yes. As soon as I get it on Friday, we'll leave.

OTTIS. Friday?

PREACHER. Yes. I'd get it sooner but Gladys might find out before we could leave town. I'm getting the money from a joint account. If I wait till Friday to get it, she won't know until at least Monday. And we'll be gone.

OTTIS. What about bank machines? Cards?

PREACHER. No, it's a money market. The only way you can get to it is through a bank teller.

OTTIS. Well, you'll have to hold on till Sunday.

PREACHER. Why Sunday?

OTTIS. Family business.

PREACHER. No. NO, I can't wait until Sunday. I'm getting the money from an account that Gladys and I have saved all these years to have a baby. And if I take it on Friday, I have to leave on Friday.

OTTIS. Before I leave town, I have to take care of something.

PREACHER. Not Sunday.

OTTIS. I'll meet you right here, Sunday night, after church.

PREACHER. No. That means I have to preach two sermons on Sunday, knowing I've stolen my wife's savings and that I'm leaving her.

OTTIS. So, Sunday morning, preach on the evils of money, and Sunday night preach on adultery.

PREACHER. Don't say that.

OTTIS. Although, I'm not sure if technically it is adultery, unless you would've had sex with a woman. I'm not sure queers are covered in that commandment.

PREACHER. Ah, Jesus.

OTTIS. Oh come on, daddy man.

PREACHER. I don't know. I have feelings. But I love Gladys.

OTTIS. Yes. Me, too.

PREACHER. What?

OTTIS. Nothing.

PREACHER. Ottis, don't get me wrong. It's not in the same way.

OTTIS. I know.

PREACHER. I don't know if I can do this.

OTTIS. It's your choice, daddy man. It's funny how things work. I came to tell you, too. I'm getting out. I'm leaving. I can't take it anymore. And you know I'm inviting you. I'll understand either way. But I've got to go. *(Ottis turns and crosses toward the front door.)*

PREACHER. But how are you going to make it? *(Ottis turns to Preacher.)*

OTTIS. Trust the Lord, daddy man. One way or another, the money will be there. *(Long pause.)* Look, go to church Sunday. Do what you've got to do. No one in town will miss you for a week.

PREACHER. I'd planned to tell Gladys, I'm going to preach a revival this week. She'll like that. She'll think I'm making money.

OTTIS. Sunday night after church.

PREACHER. Here?

OTTIS. If they don't see you go home, they'll think you're up to something. Just do what you normally do, and everything'll be fine. I'll park my pickup on the other side of that clearing, just before you get to the house. I'll cover it with brush pile. No one'll see it. *(Ottis begins to leave.)*

PREACHER. Ottis.

OTTIS. Just do what I tell you. *(Ottis exits. Preacher looks around and takes a deep breath. Gospel music rises. Blackout.)*

Scene 3

It is the following Sunday morning. Music fades, and lights up on Ottis sitting across the table from Gladys. Ottis is in the same seat he was in at the beginning of the last scene, Act Two, Scene 2. And Gladys is sitting where Preacher sat.

GLADYS. I've got something to show you.

OTTIS. Another set of *unloaded* guns?

GLADYS. I told you, I'm sorry about that. I wouldn't have blamed you if you never came back.

OTTIS. I'm leaving today.

GLADYS. New York?

OTTIS. Yes.

GLADYS. I've got a surprise.

OTTIS. What?

GLADYS. Money. And, I'm going with you.

OTTIS. What?

GLADYS. The company won't know until tomorrow.

OTTIS. Jesus.

GLADYS. Henry also goes to the bank every Monday. He'll find out tomorrow, too.

OTTIS. Find out what?

GLADYS. On Friday, after I cashed the payroll check, I withdrew half of our savings.

OTTIS. Half?

GLADYS. Yes. I can't leave Henry totally dry. He's going to need some help to get through college. He saved half of it, too. I hope you understand.

OTTIS. Jesus.

GLADYS. The money was supposed to be for me to have my baby.

OTTIS. Your baby?

GLADYS. My baby, baby. Your baby. I found out yesterday. I'm having your baby.

OTTIS. You're not.

GLADYS. Don't you say that. I am. I'm pregnant. And this time it's coming out mine.

OTTIS. Oh, Jesus.

GLADYS. I'm telling my husband today. It's not his. It's mine. And it's yours.

OTTIS. Mine?

GLADYS. I did it for us.

OTTIS. You did what for us?

GLADYS. I made sure that when you and I were together, the conditions were right.

OTTIS. What the hell are you saying?

GLADYS. Don't be mad. I did it for you.

OTTIS. You didn't do anything for me. You did it for you. You're not pregnant.

GLADYS. Yes, I am.

OTTIS. How could you be?

GLADYS. You'll see soon enough. *(Gladys exits to bedroom and brings her suitcase and a briefcase.)* Now, I can share my half of our savings with you, with a good conscience. There's no use giving it to some clinic. You did all the work.

OTTIS. Ah, Christ.

GLADYS. I thought hard about taking all the money, but I couldn't do that to Henry.

OTTIS. How much is half?

GLADYS. Ten thousand.

OTTIS. Jesus, woman.

GLADYS. Ottis, think about it. New York City. The money. Me. You. And our baby. Tonight.

OTTIS. Tonight.

GLADYS. Yes. *(Looks at watch.)* I know this won't make any sense, but I want you to pack your pickup and wait for me. As soon as my husband comes home, we'll leave. I am so ready for this, but you have to understand I do love Henry. Not in the same way I love you, of course. But please. This is not easy. I need to talk to him. It's odd. I feel like he knows something already. We've hardly spoken since Friday.

OTTIS. Oh, my God.

GLADYS. You don't want me to go, do you?

OTTIS. No, it's not that.

GLADYS. What is it?

OTTIS. It's just a lot at one time. The baby, you, your husband and all.

GLADYS. It'll be fine. I'll just say goodbye. Honey will be fine. He got a revival job. He's going away this week, too. I just have to say a proper goodbye. You can't spend your life with a man and then just leave without saying something.

OTTIS. Sure. I understand.

GLADYS. Now you take the cases. *(Gladys gives Ottis the suitcase and the briefcase.)* Ottis, you don't know how happy this makes me.

OTTIS. What about the money?

GLADYS. This is the one with the money. Eight thousand from a payroll check. I wrote an extra check from the trucking company payroll to myself.

OTTIS. Nobody asked you to steal.

GLADYS. Shut up and take it. I'll bring the rest tonight.

OTTIS. You're sure about this?

GLADYS. I've never been more sure about anything in all my life. *(Gladys kisses him.)* Now go on. Pack up. You can park your pickup on the other side of the clearing, just before you get to the house. *(Gladys pushes ... He crosses.)* Put some brush pile over the hood so no one w... Give me a few minutes with my husband and I'll meet you. *Ottis exits. Gladys takes a deep breath as lights fade down. Music up. Blackout.)*

Scene 4

Lights up on downstage right. It is dark. Ottis is standing in front of the pickup truck. The cases are on the hood. The briefcase is opened. He is counting the money. The tire well and bed of the truck are visible behind him. He has the suitcase of money opened. He is sweating. His shirt is unbuttoned. He hears a noise behind him. He closes the case. He looks around and sees nothing. He puts the money case in the truck. He reaches under the seat and pulls out a bottle of whiskey. He drinks hard. He listens. He hears nothing. He sees Gladys' suitcase on the hood. He puts the whiskey back. He grabs her case and throws it off into the woods. He hops in the truck. He picks the keys up off the dashboard. He starts to put them in the ignition. But he can't bring himself to do it. He throws the keys back on the dashboard. He takes another drink. He looks up toward the house. He takes another drink. He puts the whiskey down. He pulls a pistol out from under the seat. He hears music rise. He hears an opera. He hears lines of poetry, Gladys' voice, Preacher's voice. He hears a baby laughing. The opera and baby rise together. It gets louder. Even louder.

OTTIS. Jesus fucking Christ! *(Preacher comes around the back of the truck. He opens the passenger door, gets in, and slams the door. Simultaneously, the music stops. Preacher gets in with his bag and a large envelope.)*

PREACHER. Let's go. *(Ottis looks at him but doesn't respond.)* Come on Ottis. Let's go. *(Pause.)*

OTTIS. Did you bring the money?

PREACHER. Yes.

OTTIS. You're lying.

PREACHER. I am not. *(Ottis pulls out his pistol.)*

OTTIS. Yes you are.

PREACHER. What are you doing?

OTTIS. I don't know, Preacher. What are you doing?

PREACHER. Here it is, half our savings. I couldn't get the rest. Gladys withdrew exactly half on Friday before I got there. She's on to us. I can feel it.

OTTIS. Ah, Jesus.

PREACHER. But don't worry. I also brought the entire offering for the church for the week and all the money they took up for the new hymnals. There's close to another thousand. *(Ottis squeezes the trigger on the pistol, but he stops just short of firing it. He grits his teeth.)*

OTTIS. Nobody asked you to steal.

PREACHER. Don't call it that. Besides, it was Miss Alva's money, and they ain't nothing but a family of thieves anyway.

OTTIS. Did you go in the house and say goodbye?

PREACHER. I couldn't do it.

OTTIS. You're going to be snuffed out of her life, and you don't even have the decency to say goodbye?

PREACHER. I can't face leaving her. Come on, Ottis, and let's go before anyone finds out. *(Ottis breathes heavily and drops his pistol back between his legs. Preacher pulls out a gun.)* The gun is a good

52

idea. And it's best I get in the back, in the bed of the truck. No one will see me when we leave town. And if they do, I'll be ready. *(Preacher gets out of the cab of the truck and gets behind Ottis in the bed of the truck. Ottis sweats. He takes another drink. He again hears the music. Preacher raps on the window behind him. Muffled:)* Ottis, let's go. *(Ottis doesn't hear him. Preacher gets back down out of sight. Ottis hears opera and voices again. It gets louder. Gladys comes around the back of the truck. She opens the passenger door, climbs in with a large envelope and a gun, and she closes the door. Simultaneously, the music stops.)*

GLADYS. Ottis, let's go. I can't wait any longer. Henry is never this late. We can't wait. *(Ottis stares straight ahead.)*

OTTIS. You didn't say goodbye.

GLADYS. I wanted to tell him about our baby. *(Preacher becomes visible between Ottis and Gladys.)* I swear to God, I loved every fight with that man. *(Gladys turns slightly and is startled to see Preacher. Ottis hears music again. Gladys and Preacher stare at each other. It is now fever pitch. Ottis pulls the pistol out from between his legs. Preacher and Gladys turn and look at Ottis. He slowly turns, for the first time, and looks at both of them. He puts his pistol on them. They hold their pistols tight. They shrink back. He turns his pistol to his own head. Music rises. He grips the handle tighter and grits his teeth. He pulls the gun down. He grips the barrel and stares at it. Opera music and poetry rises along with gospel music. He puts down the gun. He takes the keys and cranks the ignition. The engine rises. He revs the engine, leaving exhaust. He turns on the headlights. They drive away. Lights fade, gospel and opera music rise higher. Blackout. Upbeat gospel song, like "I'll Fly Away," rises. Lights back up. Music continues. Preacher is now in the driver's seat. He is driving the truck. Gladys is in the passenger seat. Ottis is riding between them. They are in awe of the New York City skyline. Gladys, Ottis, and Preacher get out of the truck and come downstage for a curtain call.)*

End of Play

PROPERTY LIST

Box of tissues, blanket, compact (GLADYS)
Purse (GLADYS, OTTIS)
Towel (PREACHER, OTTIS)
Comb, shirt, tie, vest, coat (PREACHER)
Quart jars of green beans (PREACHER)
Pistols, butcher knife (GLADYS, OTTIS, PREACHER)
Bible (PREACHER)
Watch, cassette tape, shoes, earrings (GLADYS)
Box of candy, banana (OTTIS)
Tableware, food, water (GLADYS)
Whisky in a glass and bottled (GLADYS, OTTIS)
Red soda (GLADYS, PREACHER)
Bag of groceries (PREACHER)
Cans of vegetables (PREACHER)
Suitcase, briefcase (GLADYS, OTTIS)
Car keys (OTTIS)
Cash (GLADYS, PREACHER, OTTIS)
Hairbrush (GLADYS)
Cigarettes, breath spray (PREACHER)
Baggage, large envelope (PREACHER)

SOUND EFFECTS

Car starting
Grandfather clock, chimes once
Gospel music
Knock on door
Shower water
Opera
Sound montage: opera, poetry, gospel
Sound montage: characters' voices, music, baby laughter

NEW PLAYS

★ **INTIMATE APPAREL by Lynn Nottage.** The moving and lyrical story of a turn-of-the-century black seamstress whose gifted hands and sewing machine are the tools she uses to fashion her dreams from the whole cloth of her life's experiences. "…Nottage's play has a delicacy and eloquence that seem absolutely right for the time she is depicting…" –*NY Daily News.* "…thoughtful, affecting…The play offers poignant commentary on an era when the cut and color of one's dress—and of course, skin—determined whom one could and could not marry, sleep with, even talk to in public." –*Variety.* [2M, 4W] ISBN: 0-8222-2009-1

★ **BROOKLYN BOY by Donald Margulies.** A witty and insightful look at what happens to a writer when his novel hits the bestseller list. "The characters are beautifully drawn, the dialogue sparkles…" –*nytheatre.com.* "Few playwrights have the mastery to smartly investigate so much through a laugh-out-loud comedy that combines the vintage subject matter of successful writer-returning-to-ethnic-roots with the familiar mid-life crisis." –*Show Business Weekly.* [4M, 3W] ISBN: 0-8222-2074-1

★ **CROWNS by Regina Taylor.** Hats become a springboard for an exploration of black history and identity in this celebratory musical play. "Taylor pulls off a Hat Trick: She scores thrice, turning CROWNS into an artful amalgamation of oral history, fashion show, and musical theater…" –*TheatreMania.com.* "…wholly theatrical…Ms. Taylor has created a show that seems to arise out of spontaneous combustion, as if a bevy of department-store customers simultaneously decided to stage a revival meeting in the changing room." –*NY Times.* [1M, 6W (2 musicians)] ISBN: 0-8222-1963-8

★ **EXITS AND ENTRANCES by Athol Fugard.** The story of a relationship between a young playwright on the threshold of his career and an aging actor who has reached the end of his. "[Fugard] can say more with a single line than most playwrights convey in an entire script…Paraphrasing the title, it's safe to say this drama, making its memorable entrance into our consciousness, is unlikely to exit as long as a theater exists for exceptional work." –*Variety.* "A thought-provoking, elegant and engrossing new play…" –*Hollywood Reporter.* [2M] ISBN: 0-8222-2041-5

★ **BUG by Tracy Letts.** A thriller featuring a pair of star-crossed lovers in an Oklahoma City motel facing a bug invasion, paranoia, conspiracy theories and twisted psychological motives. "…obscenely exciting…top-flight craftsmanship. Buckle up and brace yourself…" –*NY Times.* "…[a] thoroughly outrageous and thoroughly entertaining play…the possibility of enemies, real and imagined, to squash has never been more theatrical." –*A.P.* [3M, 2W] ISBN: 0-8222-2016-4

★ **THOM PAIN (BASED ON NOTHING) by Will Eno.** An ordinary man muses on childhood, yearning, disappointment and loss, as he draws the audience into his last-ditch plea for empathy and enlightenment. "It's one of those treasured nights in the theater—treasured nights anywhere, for that matter—that can leave you both breathless with exhilaration and…in a puddle of tears." –*NY Times.* "Eno's words…are familiar, but proffered in a way that is constantly contradictory to our expectations. Beckett is certainly among his literary ancestors." –*nytheatre.com.* [1M] ISBN: 0-8222-2076-8

★ **THE LONG CHRISTMAS RIDE HOME by Paula Vogel.** Past, present and future collide on a snowy Christmas Eve for a troubled family of five. "…[a] lovely and hauntingly original family drama…a work that breathes so much life into the theater." –*Time Out.* "…[a] delicate visual feast…" –*NY Times.* "…brutal and lovely…the overall effect is magical." –*NY Newsday.* [3M, 3W] ISBN: 0-8222-2003-2

DRAMATISTS PLAY SERVICE, INC.
440 Park Avenue South, New York, NY 10016 212-683-8960 Fax 212-213-1539
postmaster@dramatists.com www.dramatists.com